# HABITATS
# Tropical Rainforests

## Robert Snedden

W

FRANKLIN WATTS
LONDON • SYDNEY

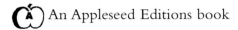 An Appleseed Editions book

First published in 2004 by Franklin Watts
96 Leonard Street, London, EC2A 4XD

Franklin Watts Australia
56 O'Riordan Street, Alexandria, NSW 2015

© 2004 Appleseed Editions

Created by Appleseed Editions Ltd,
Well House, Friars Hill, Guestling, East Sussex, TN35 4ET

Designed by Helen James

A CIP catalogue for this book is available from the British Library.

Photographs by Corbis (Brandon D. Cole, Jay Dickman, Michael & Patricia
Fogden, Galen Rowell, Kevin Schafer), Jay Ireland & Georgienne Bradley, JLM
Visuals (Richard P. Jacobs), Tom Stack & Associates (Chip & Jill Isenhart, Mark
Newman, Brian Parker, Inga Spence, Mark Allen Stack, Tom & Therisa Stack,
TSADO/NASA, Dave Watts, Tess & David Young)

Printed and bound in Thailand

# Contents

# Where are the rainforests?

The place where a living thing makes its home is called its **habitat**. A habitat can be as small as a damp place under a rotting log, or as big as the ocean. The biggest habitats, such as deserts, forests and mountains, are called **biomes**.

## Finding the forests

Forest biomes cover large areas of the Earth's land. There are several different kinds of forest biomes. One kind, tropical rainforest, circles the planet around its middle like a green belt. Tropical rainforests grow in places where the temperatures are always high and where a lot of rain falls throughout the year. Close to the **equator**,

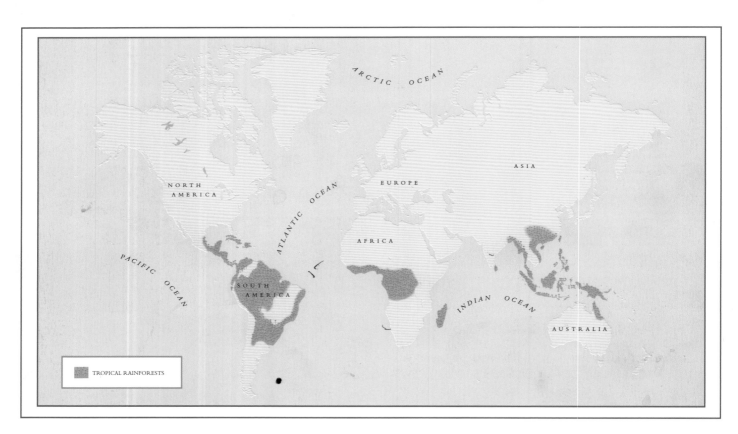

TROPICAL RAINFORESTS

*Tropical rainforests form a green band around the **equatorial** regions of Earth.*

in Asia, Africa and Central and South America, the conditions are right for tropical rainforests to grow.

The largest rainforest in the world grows around the Amazon River in South America. This rainforest alone makes up almost half the world's rainforest habitat. In Africa, rainforests grow around the Congo River of West Africa and near the coast of the Atlantic Ocean. There is also a rainforest on the east coast of the island of Madagascar. The rainforests of Asia grow in two main areas. One area includes Malaysia, the islands of Borneo and the Philippines. The other covers large areas of the island of New Guinea and parts of northern Australia.

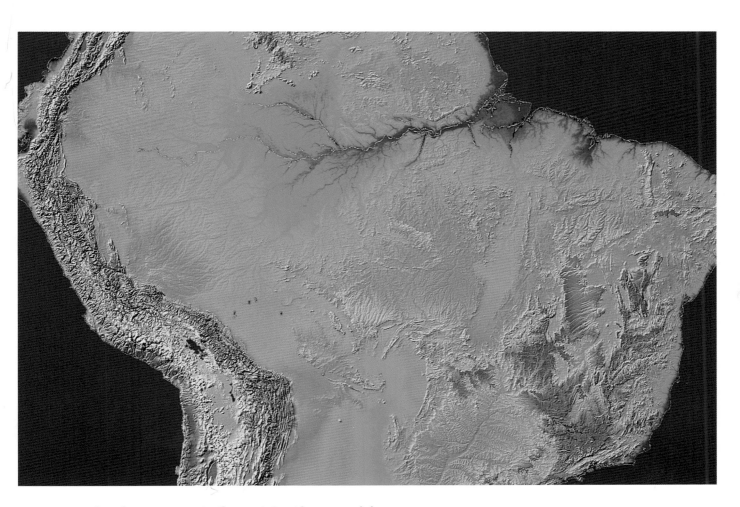

▲ *The largest rainforest in the world grows around the Amazon River of South America.*

5

# Rainforest weather

On a typical day in a rainforest, the weather is likely to be hot and steamy. The temperature doesn't change much over the course of the year near the equator. It rarely falls below a warm 20° Celsius and doesn't often rise above 34° Celsius.

▲ The leaves on rainforest trees have pointed drip-tips to help water run off them.

## Cloud forests

True rainforests do not grow above 1,000 metres because the temperature drops as **altitude** increases. High on tropical mountains, the trees are small and covered with mosses and ferns. These woods are called elfinwoods or cloud forests, and they are like miniature rainforests.

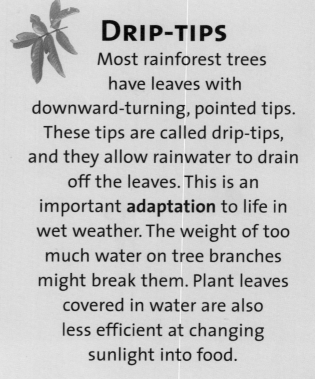

### DRIP-TIPS
Most rainforest trees have leaves with downward-turning, pointed tips. These tips are called drip-tips, and they allow rainwater to drain off the leaves. This is an important **adaptation** to life in wet weather. The weight of too much water on tree branches might break them. Plant leaves covered in water are also less efficient at changing sunlight into food.

▲ *Huge amounts of water evaporate from the leaves of rainforest trees.*

## Wet, wet, wet!

There are no dry seasons in a true rainforest. It is wet all the year round. As little as 200 centimetres or as much as 900 centimetres of rain may fall over a year. Usually, at least 20 centimetres of rain falls every month in a rainforest. By comparison, even the wettest parts of rainy Great Britain rarely have more than 150 centimetres of rain during a year.

## Living weather machines

Half the rain that falls on the Amazon rainforest blows in from the Atlantic Ocean. The rest is produced by the trees of the forest. Trees are like giant, living water pumps, bringing up moisture from the ground. This moisture is lost through the leaves of the trees by **evaporation**. The moist air from the trees' leaves rises up above the forest. When it hits colder air, the rising moist air forms clouds, and the water falls back to the Earth as rain.

# Living in layers

The rainforest is divided into different layers, like a multi-storey block of flats. Each layer has its own distinctive characteristics and creatures.

## Life at the top

Standing proudly above the forest **canopy** are the emergent trees — the giants of the forest. They have massive trunks more than 2 metres across and grow to 35-70 metres or more. The emergents are widely spaced and have umbrella-shaped tops. Fast-flying birds and bats swoop between the treetops.

## On the roof

The trees that form the canopy of the rainforest are 20-30 metres tall. They have dense, leafy crowns, or tops, that absorb most of the sunlight, and prevent it reaching the layers below. Vast numbers of animals make their homes in the canopy.

*Flowers in the rainforest are **pollinated** by a variety of insects, animals and birds, including hummingbirds. Without these creatures, many plants could not reproduce.*

emergent trees

canopy

understorey

forest floor

 *Many different types of trees grow in the rainforest, forming distinct layers. Emergent trees stand out above the canopy below.*

## Going down

The next level down is the understorey. It is very damp and warm, with very little light. The plants that grow in the understorey have very large leaves to collect as much light as possible. Understorey trees tend to be about 10-15 metres tall. The crowns of the trees are tightly packed together, but growth is sparse below, and animals can move easily between the trees. Flowers in the understorey are brightly-coloured and have strong scents. These adaptations allow them to attract insects, birds and bats in the dim light.

## Ground floor

The ground level of a tropical rainforest is also warm, damp and dark. The air is still. Unlike the environment portrayed in some films set in the jungle, few plants grow on the rainforest floor. Only on the edge of the forest or along the banks of rivers is there enough light for a lot of plants to grow.

Leaves and animal droppings from the layers above drop down to the forest floor. There they rot quickly and are consumed, or eaten, by huge numbers of ants, termites and other minibeasts. In a short time, a rich **compost** forms, providing **nutrients** that are taken up by the many tree roots.

# Rainforest recycling

Rainforests seem to be incredibly **fertile** places. There is more living material in a square kilometre of rainforest than there is in the same space in any other habitat. However, although the forest is productive, it grows on very poor soil. Rainforest soils can't hold nutrients in the same way that soils in cooler climates can. High temperatures and heavy rainfall remove the nutrients from the soil. So how do rainforests manage to grow so well?

*Clearing the forest makes the land unproductive, as most of the nutrients in a rainforest are stored within the trees.*

## Little helpers

The high temperatures of the rainforest floor provide ideal growing conditions for bacteria. These microscopic organisms are among the rainforest trees' most important helpers.

Any leaves, animal droppings or other materials which fall to the floor from the trees above are swiftly consumed by ants and other small animals. This is the first step in the rainforest **recycling** process.

## STILT SUPPORTS

Rainforest trees have such shallow roots that they often need other means of support. Some trees have stilt roots that split off from the tree a few centimetres above the ground. These roots make the tree more stable, and also allow it to take more nutrients from the soil. Other trees have large outgrowths at the base, called buttresses, that spread the weight of the tree over a larger area.

*Some rainforest trees have stilt roots to give them extra support.*

The bacteria then continue the process begun by the minibeasts. Together, they quickly break down the leaves and other remains. In this way, the bacteria release the nutrients in the droppings and make them available for the trees to use again.

The trees and the bacteria need each other to survive. The trees provide a source of food for the bacteria in the form of falling leaves, and the bacteria break down the leaves to provide the nutrients the trees need.

## Tree stores

In the cooler forests of **temperate climates**, trees can take nutrients as they need them from the soil. In the rainforest, however, trees have to compete with each other for nutrients as well as for light. Rainforest trees have shallow roots that spread out over a wide area, unlike the deeply growing roots of temperate forest trees. Rainforest tree roots grab nutrients from the soil as soon as they become available, and they are stored in the living bodies of the trees.

# Life at ground level

There is little food for plant-eating animals at ground level in the rainforest because few plant grow there. Most animals are small- to medium-sized and feed on fruits and seeds that fall to the ground. Big **mammals** are less common in the rainforest because of the lack of food, but there are a few. Examples include the elephants of Africa and Asia, the pygmy hippo and the gorilla of Africa, and the tapir of South America.

## Seed and fruit collectors

In rainforests all over the world, there are animals that feed on nothing but fallen fruits and seeds. The African rainforests are home to small antelopes called duikers. There are several varieties of duikers.

Each kind is adapted to feed on a unique type of seed or fruit. One kind of duiker has teeth that can crack the hardest seed. Another has a flexible jaw that allows it to eat some of the largest fruits.

*The blue duiker of Africa is one of the world's smallest antelopes, and stands less than 40 centimetres tall at the shoulder.*

Agoutis are cat-sized rodents that live in the rainforests of South America. These seed collectors perform a valuable service for the rainforest trees. They collect seeds and hide them to be eaten later. Often, the seeds are not eaten at all. Instead, they **germinate**, thanks to the animals, far from the parent tree. This ensures that different varieties of trees are scattered throughout the rainforest.

## Pigs in the woods

Wild pigs are found in rainforests around the world. They root, or dig, for food in the soil with their snouts and eat plant roots, insects and small animals. Pig herds defend their territory and attack other animals that stray into it, including unwary human travellers.

*South American tapirs are nocturnal plant-eaters, which means they feed at night.*

### ELEPHANT CLEARINGS

African forest elephants are sometimes called the architects of the rainforest. They create clearings in the forest around drinking holes. These clearings can be 100 metres or more across. Young plants cannot establish themselves because the elephants trample or eat them. Asian elephants play a similar role in the rainforests of India and South-east Asia.

13

# Understorey life

The understorey isn't quite as dark as the forest floor, but it is still fairly dim. This level of the forest is made up of smaller trees, shrubs and vines.

Understorey trees have special adaptations that allow them to thrive in dim light. Some trees grow flowers on their trunks, where they are easily spotted by pollinating birds and insects. The flowers often have strong scents as well to attract pollinators.

## Forest disguises

Tree flowers want to be seen easily, but rainforest animals often have adaptations that keep them hidden. Most of the **reptiles** that

### HOME RAINFOREST

Many plants from the understorey, such as zebra plants, are now common houseplants. They need very little sunlight or water, so understorey plants are well-suited to life in people's homes.

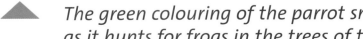
*The green colouring of the parrot snake camouflages it as it hunts for frogs in the trees of the Amazon rainforest.*

The South American red-eyed tree frog clings securely to the leaves and branches of the trees.

live in the understorey are **camouflaged** to blend in with the background. The emerald tree boa's bright green colour, for example, makes it difficult for eagles to see against the tree leaves. The disguise also helps the boa sneak up unseen on unsuspecting **prey**.

Larger animals can be hard to see in the forest, too. The jaguar's spots camouflage it in the dappled light falling through the leaves.

## Forest frogs

The damp conditions of the understorey are just right for **amphibians** such as salamanders and frogs. Amphibians need water to lay their eggs in and to stop their skin drying out. Tree frogs' feet have tiny suction pads covered with a sticky

## NOT SO FAST!

The three-toed sloth is very well adapted to life in the branches of the South American rainforest. It avoids drawing the attention of predators such as the jaguar by moving so slowly that it isn't noticed. It is also well disguised, thanks to a simple green plant, called an alga, that lives in its fur, making the brown sloth appear green!

substance. This adaptation helps them grip tree branches and move swiftly to escape **predators**.

15

# Tops of the trees

The canopy, or overstorey, of the rainforest is an almost continuous layer of tree crowns. This is a mysterious place, hard to reach and full of life. The canopy varies from forest to forest. South America's forest treetops are bound together by plants and vines, African forest canopies are umbrella-shaped and Asian forest trees have narrow crowns.

## Dazzling diversity

There is a tremendous variety of living things in the rainforest habitat. About nine out of ten of the living things in the rainforest live in the canopy. Some scientists believe that half the world's animal species live in rainforest canopies.

The sun shines brightest in the canopy. Vines, trees and other plants compete for the light. There is an abundance of flowers and fruits and leaves, which offer a great deal to eat. There are so many layers of plants on which animals can swing, climb

*The toucan is one of the many birds of the rainforest canopy. It uses its colourful beak to peel fruit and to catch young birds and insects.*

*Sugar glider females carry their young in pouches.*

their hind feet. Their sharp claws also make them excellent climbers. Another glider is the flying squirrel. There are more than 40 different types of flying squirrels, and many live in the world's rainforests. They can glide over distances of more than 50 metres between trees. There are even flying frogs! They leap from tree to tree, spreading apart their long, webbed toes to glide through the air for distances of 15 metres or so.

and scurry that they can spend their whole lives in the treetops and never touch the ground. There are frogs, for example, that breed in the pools of water that collect in the plants growing on the trees.

Animals that can fly are perfectly adapted for treetop life. Birds, bats and insects are abundant in the canopy. There are also large numbers of climbing animals, such as monkeys, squirrels and lizards.

## Gliders

Some animals can't fly from tree to tree, but they can glide. One such animal is the sugar glider, found in the rainforests of New Guinea, Indonesia and Australia. These tiny animals are a type of possum. They glide through the trees on a sail-like skin flap that stretches from their front to

## DON'T TOUCH
Canopy trees in a rainforest do not actually touch one another. There are gaps between the trees. Scientists call this canopy shyness, and no one knows exactly why it happens.

# Tree climbers

**N**ot all the plants that climb towards the light in the forest are trees or shrubs. Many other plants use the trees for support as they compete with them for light. These highly adapted plants grow only in rainforests.

## Climbing together

Lianas often start life as shrubs firmly rooted in the forest floor. As they grow, they put out long branches that attach themselves to the trunks of nearby trees or to tree saplings. The lianas and the trees climb together until they reach the sunlight at the roof of the forest. There the lianas produce large crowns of leaves and flowers. Almost half the leaves in the forest canopy belong to lianas rather than trees. Lianas often produce **aerial roots**, which can absorb moisture from the air.

## Tree trunk plants

Epiphytes are another type of plant that relies on trees for support. Unlike lianas, they are not rooted in the ground. Instead, they grow on tree trunks or in the crooks of branches. Epiphytes do not take any nutrients from the host tree, which only provides them with a place to grow. They have small, sticky roots that help them to grip the tree. Some rely almost entirely on collecting rainwater as a source of minerals. Bromeliads, such as the pineapple plant, form a cup-shaped rosette of thick, waxy, waterproof leaves that can store more than 30 litres of water. Many types of orchids and ferns are epiphytes.

*Lianas are woody climbers that cling to the rainforest trees with long, hooked branches.*

*Orchids are the most common type of epiphyte – plants that grow on other plants.*

## Stranglers

Some epiphytes eventually become stranglers. At a certain point in their growth, they produce aerial roots that wrap around the trunk of the tree as they make their way down towards the ground. The increased supply of nutrients the plant takes in this way allows it to grow more strongly. Its branches soon spread upwards into the canopy, competing with the tree for sunlight. Eventually, the strangler's roots completely surround the tree and kill it. When the dead tree trunk collapses, the strangler's strong network of roots – stretching from the canopy to the forest floor – continues to support the plant.

# Monkeying around

Monkeys are some of the most common inhabitants of the rainforest canopy. They are superbly adapted to forest life, moving confidently through the branches and feasting on fruits, nuts, leaves and berries.

## New World monkeys

Monkeys are divided into two groups, according to which part of the world they live in. Old World monkeys live in Africa and Asia. New World monkeys live in Central and South America.

Most New World monkeys belong to a family that includes the squirrel, spider, woolly and capuchin monkeys. New World monkeys live everywhere in the rainforest, from the forest floor to the top of the canopy. Most are fairly large. The largest, the woolly spider monkey, weighs more than 15 kilograms. Many New World

monkeys are very sociable. The squirrel monkey, for example, roams the trees in troops of up to 500 monkeys.

Tamarins and marmosets also belong to the New World monkey group. They are

The howler monkey has an amazingly loud call that can be heard several kilometres away.

### A CHORUS OF HOWLS

The howler monkey is one of the largest New World monkeys. Howlers defend their territories in the forest canopy by producing extraordinarily loud, deep, throaty calls. A howler chorus can be heard more than 5 kilometres away.

 *The langurs of Asia are among the largest of the Old World monkeys.*

small monkeys. Some are about the size of house cats, while others are no bigger than rats. Their tails are often longer than the rest of their bodies. Marmosets leap with great agility between tree branches, whereas tamarins tend to climb straight up and down.

## Strong tails

Many New World monkeys have strong tails that are mostly hairless underneath and covered with touch-sensitive pads. They are called called **prehensile tails**, and monkeys use them as an extra limb to grip branches when they are climbing through the trees.

## Old World monkeys

Some types of Old World monkeys live in tropical rainforests, but others live in grasslands and even in mountainous areas. Typical Old World rainforest monkeys include the colobus monkeys of Africa and the macaques and langurs of Asia. Most are quite big – about the size of an average dog. The Hanuman langur, for example, has a metre-long body.

Many monkeys have cheek pouches that expand like a hamster's to store food. This is useful for monkeys that compete for food and don't like to share. No New World monkeys have pouches, and no Old World monkeys have a prehensile tail.

# Apes of the forest

The apes are humans' closest relatives in the animal world. The great apes include the chimpanzee, the bonobo and gorilla of Africa, and the orangutan of Indonesia. Gibbons, which live in South-east Asia and Indonesia, are smaller and are sometimes called the lesser apes.

The orangutans of Indonesia are highly intelligent animals, as well as agile climbers.

## Orangutans

The word orangutan means 'man of the forest' in the language of Malasia and Indonesia. These great apes live in a range of forest habitats on the islands of Borneo and Sumatra. Full-grown male orangutans can weigh around 100 kilograms. Female orangutans are much smaller.

Orangutans have a varied diet that includes leaves, bark, flowers, fruit, ants, termites and birds' eggs. Big though they are, orangutans spend most of their time in the trees, swinging effortlessly on their long, powerful arms. Every night they make a new nest, complete with roof, in a tree.

## Chimpanzees

Chimpanzees live in the forests and grasslands of equatorial Africa. Male chimpanzees weigh about 80 kilograms and stand about a metre tall. Females are smaller.

Bonobos, or pygmy chimpanzees, live in central Africa. They look

*Long-armed gibbons swing from branch to branch with ease.*

very much like chimpanzees, except that they are shorter, with longer limbs and a more upright posture. Bonobos have black coats and shiny black faces.

Both bonobos and chimpanzees build nests in trees to sleep in every night. Both eat just about anything they can get their hands on, including honey, leaves, fruit, ants, birds' eggs, birds, smaller mammals and reptiles.

## Gorillas

Gorillas live in the forests of equatorial Africa. A full-grown male gorilla can weigh 150 kilograms or more. Females are usually smaller. Adult males are often called silverbacks because as they grow older, the hair on their backs turns from black to silver. Despite their size, gorillas are shy animals. They live in small groups of between five and fifiteen animals with one silverback leader. Gorillas eat plants, berries and leaves every day. At night they build a camp where the group sleeps. The females and their young make nests in the tree branches, while the males sleep under the tree.

## Gibbons

Gibbons are the real kings of the swingers, moving with ease from branch to branch on their long, slim arms. They are the smallest of the ape family and live in the forests of South-east Asia and Indonesia. Pairs of gibbons often sing bird-like, warbling duets in the morning.

# A multitude of minibeasts

One thing that all rainforests around the world have in common is the countless insects and other minibeasts that crawl, scuttle, walk and fly through every part of the forest.

## Bugs in their billions

There are probably more than 50 million different types of insects and other minibeasts living in rainforests. A single rainforest tree might be home to more than 1,200 different kinds of beetles!

Minibeasts help to keep the forest healthy. In the soil, earthworms, termites and other tiny animals feed on the remains of plants, breaking them down into small particles that can be recycled by bacteria and fungi. Countless colourful butterflies fly through the forest air, playing a vital role as plant pollinators.

▼ *Most giant spiders live on grasshoppers and other insects, although they occasionally catch and eat small birds.*

◄ *Rainforest centipedes are powerful enough to take on frogs and lizards.*

## Big bugs

Some very large insects live in the rainforest. Beetles in the forests of South America may reach 16 centimetres in length. Rainforest centipedes 20 centimentres long kill their prey with poisonous claws that can inflict a nasty bite on an unwary human explorer, too. The hairy bird-eating spiders of South America can measure 25 centimetres across.

## Ant antics

The animal that really deserves to be treated with respect in the rainforest is the ant – and there are an awful lot of them! Rainforest ants have ferociously painful bites and stings.

Leafcutter ants are common in rainforests around the world. **Foraging** parties of ants snip out bits of leaves with their strong jaws and carry them back to their nests. Foraging ants are protected by soldier ants that may weigh 300 times more than them. Even tinier leafcutters ride on top of the leaves, keeping an eye out for flies that may lay eggs on the leafcutters' leaves.

### NOW YOU SEE IT...

Many rainforest insects have incredible camouflage that allows them to hide from other animals that may try to eat them. There are insects that look like dead leaves, living leaves, half-eaten leaves, twigs, bark and flower parts.

25

# Hunters of the forest

Large prey animals are scarce in the rainforest, so large predators are scarce, too. However, the predators that live there are among the most spectacular in the world.

## Top cats

The biggest hunters that prowl the forest floor are cats. Asia has the tiger, South America the jaguar, and Africa the leopard. All these cats are formidable hunters. Because large prey animals are often hard to find, the cats are specially adapted to eat smaller ones. The jaguar, for example, is an excellent swimmer and skilled at catching fish. It also eats frogs and turtles.

The rainforest is also home to smaller cats such as the margay and ocelot of South America and the leopard cat of Asia. These animals are generally not much bigger than a house cat or dog. Most hunt at night, both on the forest floor and up in the canopy.

## Civet cats

The best-known member of the family of small, catlike hunters called civet cats is the mongoose. Several different types of mongooses live in

*Tigers are the top predators in the rainforests of India.*

a variety of habitats across Africa, the Middle East and India. They eat snakes, small mammals, birds and insects. They crack open eggs by banging them against rocks.

Another interesting member of the civet cat family is the fishing genet. Although it likes fish, the genet is a poor swimmer and doesn't like to get wet. It taps its paw on the surface of the water of forest streams to attract fish. The genet lays its long, sensitive whiskers against the surface of the water. Only when it picks up the vibrations of a passing fish does it plunge swiftly into the water to make its catch.

*The long-snouted sloth bear lives in India and Sri Lanka.*

## Bears in the trees

Sloth bears live in the tropical rainforests of Sri Lanka and southern India. They are among the most specialized of the bear family, as they are adapted for a life in the trees. The sloth bear is a large, black, shaggy animal. Its long, curved claws allow it to hang beneath branches like a real sloth. The sloth bear has a long snout, sensitive lips and a long tongue. All these adaptations help the sloth bear suck up its favourite meal – termites.

## AERIAL HUNTER

The Philippine eagle, or monkey-eating eagle, is an awesome predator. It is roughly a metre tall, with a wingspan of 2 metres. Its long tail and broad wings are superbly adapted for swift flight among the trees. It has a massive, powerful beak and strong, clawed legs. Lemurs, squirrels, snakes, civet cats, bats and even monkeys fall victim to this rainforest hunter.

# The threatened forest

The amazing plants and wildlife of the rainforest are under threat. The danger to the world's rainforests comes from the activities of humans.

*Removing trees from the rainforest for timber is incredibly destructive.*

## Cutting down the forests

**Deforestation** is the destruction of a forest for **timber** or fuel, or to clear the land for farming. People argue about how fast the forests are disappearing, but at least 32,000 hectares of forest probably disappear from the Earth every day. This means that over 15 years an area the size of Mexico is lost. As the forest disappears, so too do the animals that depend upon it.

Many animals vanish into **extinction** without ever having been observed or named. As the forests are destroyed, more carbon dioxide, a **greenhouse gas**, is added to the air, possibly altering climates around the world.

*As populations grow and cities become bigger, more pressure is put on the rainforest.*

## Farmers and ranchers

Poor farmers in rainforest countries can't afford to buy good farmland. Instead, they clear the rainforest to grow their crops. Ranchers also clear large areas of rainforest to make pasture for their cattle. These farmers soon find that the land they have cleared cannot support healthy growth, because most of the nutrients in a rainforest are stored in the trees. Within a few years, it will grow no more crops. So the farmers move on to another patch of forest and continue the cycle.

## Logging

The rainforest is also a source of timber. Loggers cutting down trees are responsible for much destruction. Large areas of rainforest are destroyed to remove only a few logs. The heavy machinery used to build roads into the forest and to transport the timber causes a great deal of damage. It compacts the soil, making it harder for new plants to grow. The rainforest trees are connected by a network of lianas and other climbers, which means that cutting down one tree can bring down several others that are attached to it.

## What can be done?

For the huge areas of rainforest that have already disappeared, it is too late. The plants and animals that have been lost can never be put back. But people all around the world can help to save what's left. They can decide not to buy products made from rainforest hardwood trees, such as mahogany. They can also **boycott** pet shops that sell parrots, monkeys and other endangered rainforest animals as pets. We all need to recognize that rainforests are important to the whole world. **Developed countries** could offer money, education or other kinds of help to poorer countries to help save the remaining forests. One idea might be to offer farmers low-cost loans that would allow them to buy non-rainforest land, and then to buy their products at a fair price. Only by working together will the world's people be able to protect the rainforests – the Earth's priceless, living treasures.

# Glossary

**adaptation** A characteristic of a living thing that allows it to survive in its environment. Drip tips, for example, are an adaptation that allow rainforest leaves to shed water.

**aerial roots** Roots that project from the part of a plant's stem above ground.

**altitude** Height above the ground or sea level.

**amphibians** Types of animals, such as frogs and toads, with soft, moist skin, that spend at least part of their lives in water.

**biomes** Large areas of the environment with distinctive climates and plant types; examples include forests, mountains and deserts.

**boycott** To refuse to buy from or use something as a protest against it.

**camouflaged** Made difficult to see because it is the same colour or shape as the background.

**canopy** The topmost part of the forest trees; the roof of the forest.

**compost** Plant and animal remains that have been rotted down by the actions of minibeasts and microorganisms.

**deforestation** Cutting down trees from woods and forests for fuel or other purposes, or clearing an area for grazing or building.

**developed countries** Countries with economies based on industry rather than agriculture, for example Great Britain and the USA.

**equator** An imaginary line that runs around the middle of the earth, dividing it into the northern and southern hemispheres.

**equatorial** Related to the equator.

**evaporation** The process in which a liquid changes into a vapour (or gas) without boiling. Puddles of rainwater disappear as they evaporate in sunshine.

**extinction** The disappearance of an entire species of living things from the world when the last members die.

**fertile** Able to support growth. Fertile soil produces abundant plant growth.

**foraging** Searching for something to eat.

**germinate** To start to grow. When a seed grows and produces its first root and leaves, it has germinated.

**greenhouse gas** A type of gas in the atmosphere that traps heat as it rises from the surface of the Earth, like the glass in a greenhouse. This makes the atmosphere warmer than if the heat escaped into space.

**habitat** The place where a living thing makes its home; the environment that it is adapted to survive in.

**mammals** Animals that are warm-blooded and usually have hair on their skins, including humans and monkeys. Female mammals produce milk to feed their young.

**nutrients** Another word for food – all the things needed for a balanced diet to provide energy and raw materials for the growth and maintenance of an organism.

**pollinated** When pollen grains are carried to one flower from another it is pollinated. After this has happened, seeds start to form.

**predators** Animals that catch and eat other animals for food.

**prehensile tails** Tails that can be used for grasping objects.

**prey** Animals that are caught and eaten by predators.

**recycling** Reusing waste materials.

**reptiles** Cold-blooded animals, including snakes and lizards, with a dry, scaly skin. Most lay soft-shelled eggs and live on land.

**temperate climates** Areas where the weather is rarely, if ever, extremely cold or extremely hot.

**timber** Wood that is used for building.

# Index